Jane Yolen

# Welcome to the
# SEA OF SAND

*illustrated by Laura Regan*

SCHOLASTIC INC.
New York Toronto London Auckland Sydney

## Pronunciation Guide

| | |
|---|---|
| **cholla** | *cho*-yah |
| **gambel's quail** | gamble's quail |
| **gilas** | *hee*-lahs |
| **mesquite** | meh-skeet |
| **ocelot** | ah-se-lot |
| **ocotillo** | oh-ko-*tee*-yoh |
| **saguaro** | sah-wá-roh |
| **tarantula** | tah-ranch-uh-lah |

*Thank you to Pattie Fowler of the Arizona-Sonora Desert Museum for
the wonderful help and information that she provided for this book.*

ISBN 0-590-63617-0

12 11 10 9 8 7 6 5 4 3 2 1          7 8 9/9 0 1 2/0

Printed in the U.S.A.          14

First Scholastic printing, April 1997

The paintings in this book were executed in gouache on illustration board.

To Beth Meacham and Tappan King,
who introduced me to the Sonora Desert
before and after the rain          —J. Y.

With love for my husband, Peter,
who was with me every step of the way
                                    —L. R.

*"Where and how did we gain the idea that
the desert was merely a sea of sand?"*
                    —John C. Van Dyke, *The Desert*

Welcome to the sea of sand,
a hot sea,
a dry sea,
a rock and stone and sky sea,
where mountains rise like islands
high
above the waves of sand.

But this sandscape
is not just a tan scape!
It's a wash of blue sky,
the splash of terra-cotta sunrise,
the dash of a speckled roadrunner,

a cache of kangaroo rats busy in their burrows,
a scuttle of tarantulas,
a muddle of centipedes,

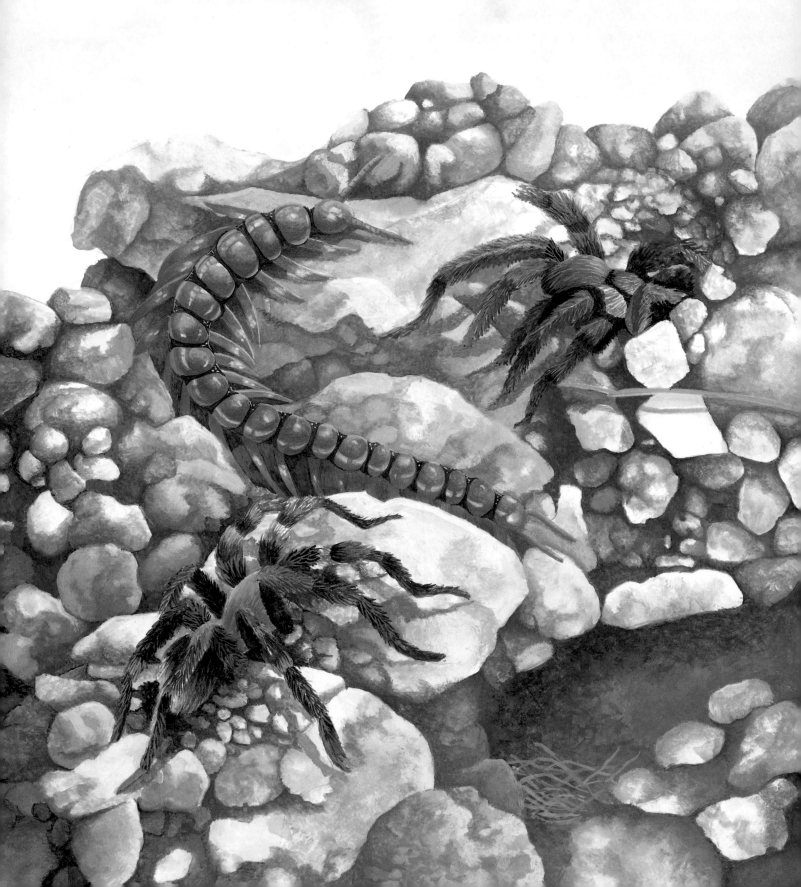

a huddle of ocelots at noon
in the shadow of a cave,

a slither of green lizards,
the dither of butterflies
hovering over the desert
surprise
landscape after rain.

And—oh!—the colors then:
the spray of ocotillo;
the play of poppies in a field;
the long green fingers of mesquite;

the sea greens, pea greens,
free greens, tea greens
of greasewood and paloverde,
brittlebush and cholla
overlooked by rams;

and blossoms following cavities,
cracks,
and folds
of land where water at last holds
seeds to their year-old vows.
And this is not a silent sea:
you can hear the yawning growl
of a mountain lion up
from his morning drowse;

the laughing call of a gambel's quail;

the late-night wail
of coyote on the trail;

the bleat of spadefoot toads;
the *hissssssss* of gilas;

the whirring *ra-tat-a-tattle* rattle
of a diamondback
warning you off his private track;

and the soft *coo-coo-roo*
of the white-winged dove
standing above
the sea of sand
in its thorny bower
of twenty-four-hour
saguaro flowers.

Welcome to the sand sea,
all-colors-of-the-band sea,
a hot sea,
a dry sea,
green-bush, red-rock, blue-sky sea.
Welcome to the desert
and the rich Sonora land.

The following birds and animals which are not mentioned in the text appear in the illustrations:

| jacket | collared lizards |
| pages 6 and 7 | desert tortoise |
| pages 12 and 13 | prairie dogs, elf owl |
| pages 14 and 15 | humming birds |
| pages 24 and 25 | scorpion |
| pages 30 and 31 | Harris' hawk |

## Did You Know?

The definition of a desert is a place where little rain falls. Deserts cover fourteen percent of the world's land surface.

But just because something is called a desert does not mean that it is deserted. Desert landscapes teem with life: plants, trees, shrubs, birds, insects, and some of the most wonderful animals on the planet roam the sand-and-scrub landscapes. The Sonora Desert, which this book describes, is one of the richest botanical and zoological areas in the world.

But the desert is a place of contradictions. Temperatures may range from below freezing in some places to *well* above 100° Fahrenheit in others. There are rivers in the desert that run swiftly, rivers that run dry in summer, and places where there is virtually no water at all.

To learn more about the Sonora Desert, which covers southwest Arizona, southeast California, most of Baja California, and the state of Sonora in Mexico, get in touch with:

Arizona-Sonora Desert Museum
2021 North Kinney Road
Tucson, Arizona 85743